AUSTRALIA IN HISTORY

The Peace Keepers: Australia at War Since 1945

A.K. Macdougall

The Five Mile Press

The Five Mile Press Pty Ltd
1 Centre Road, Scoresby
Victoria 3179 Australia
www.fivemile.com.au

Edited by Samone Bos
Designed by Sylvia Witte

First published 2004
Reprinted 2009

Printed in China 5 4 3 2 1

National Library of Australia Cataloguing-in-Publication data
Macdougall, A. K. (Anthony Keith), 1943– .
The peacekeepers: Australia at war.
Includes index.
For lower to middle secondary students.
ISBN 978 1 74124 091 7.

1. Vietnamese Conflict, 1961–1975 – Australia – Juvenile literature. 2. Iraq War, 2003 – Australia – Juvenile literature. 3. Persian Gulf War, 1991 – Juvenile literature. 4. Peacekeeping forces – Australia – Juvenile literature. 5. East Timor – History – Autonomy and independence movements – Juvenile literature. I. Title. (Series: Australia in History).

355.020994

The photographs in this book came mostly from the author's archives.

The following images are reproduced courtesy of the Australian War Memorial, Canberra: page 6; page 8 (AWM photo 146970); page 9 (AWM photo 78745); page 17 (top left), (AWM photo Col/67/325/VN); page 20 (AWM photo Bel/69/382/VN).
Pages 10; 14; 15; 19; 22 and cover (bottom middle); 25 (lower) and cover (far left); 26 and cover (bottom left); 27 (top) and cover (middle); are reproduced courtesy of the Army Public Relations and Department of Defence. Page 17 (lower) is reproduced courtesy of the Navy Public Relations.
Page 18 is an official U.S. Army photo. Page 25 (top) is reproduced courtesy of the NSW Police. Page 11 is reproduced courtesy of the US Information Service. Page 27 (lower), David Guttenfelder/AP/AAP Image; page 28 and cover (right), Abaca/AAP Image; page 29, JPAU/Australian Defence/AAP Image; page 30, Wally Santana/AP/AAP Image; page 31 and cover (bottom right), Luke Frazza/AFP/AAP Image.

Contents

The ruins of war: The world in 1945

The Second World War had devastated the world. At the war's end in 1945 Europe was in ruins, and so were the European empires in Asia that had fallen in 1942 to the Japanese. Hardly a city in Germany had survived the **Allied** bombing. For a period its people faced starvation. Twelve million refugees and former slave workers – 'Displaced Persons' – had to be cared for. The **Nazi** leaders were put on trial at Nuremberg in 1946 for crimes against humanity and many of them were sentenced to death. Britain and France had gone to war in 1939 to protect Poland from Germany, but Poland was now under harsh Soviet rule. Having lost more than 20 million people in the war against Nazi Germany, Russia now occupied Eastern Germany and was determined to keep its old enemy weak and divided.

Early in 1946, Winston Churchill, who had lost prime ministership in Britain's first post-war elections, warned that an 'iron curtain' had fallen across the face of Europe. The chill in relations between Russia and **the West** became a 'Cold War' that would last until the fall of the **Communist** nations in 1989. The Cold War was fought not in Europe but in Asia, Africa, the Middle East and Central America, where newly emerging Communist regimes often dissolved into conflict. The cost in human lives would run into the millions.

The birth of the United Nations

Australia was one of the first of the 25 Allied nations whose representatives gathered in Washington on 1 January 1942 to sign the 'Declaration of the United Nations', pledging to fight on until victory was achieved over the tyranny of the **Axis** powers.

When this victory was achieved in 1945, the Allies decided to convert their alliance into a new world government: the United Nations Organization (UNO) in which all nations in the world could be members. The major Allied powers – the United States, Britain, Soviet Russia, France and China – decided to form a 'Security Council' which had the power to authorise the use of armed forces by the UN's member nations to halt aggression. A single member of the Security Council, however,

President Truman (far left) witnesses the signing of the United Nations Charter in San Francisco in 1945.

can use the **veto** to halt any effective UN action.

By late 1946, the bulk of America's great armed forces of 15 million men were demobilised and only token forces remained in Europe. The European nations themselves were devastated, political unrest was rising, food was short and fuel was lacking.

In eastern Europe, Russian armies remained at full strength and Communist regimes were established not only in Eastern Germany but in Poland, Hungary, Yugoslavia, Romania, Bulgaria and Albania. Czechoslovakia became Communist in February 1948. Latvia, Lithuania and Estonia had been reabsorbed into the Soviet Union. It was feared that Italy and France would also fall to Communism.

The Cold War: First crisis

In February 1947, Britain informed the United States that it would have to withdraw its troops from Greece, where the royalist government was fighting a losing war with Communist **guerillas**. Turkey was also facing threats from the Soviets. America's President Truman decided to act. In March 1947, Truman announced that the United States would give massive military and economic aid to Greece and Turkey, and to any nation faced by a '**totalitarian** threat'. The Truman Doctrine was the first act to deter further expansion by Soviet Russia. In June 1947, the United States announced the 'Marshall Plan' – a project to help Europe's recovery by giving its shattered nations aid to the value of US$12,000 million over a four-year period. It marked the economic rebirth of western Europe.

In June 1948, the Russians cut road access from the western zone of Germany to Allied-occupied West Berlin in an effort to force the West out of the city, but the Americans, British and French responded with an airlift of food and fuel to Berlin. After 11 months, the Russians lifted the blockade.

In April 1949, the United States sponsored the North Atlantic Treaty Organization (NATO) which brought most of western Europe together in a mutual defence pact. When Western Germany joined NATO in 1955, the Soviet bloc responded with the Warsaw Pact. The NATO Pact still exists, and few at the time would have predicted that 50 years later former Communist countries would be applying for NATO membership.

The atomic age: An American atomic bomb test at Bikini Atoll in the Pacific in 1946.

The atomic age

In September 1949, Russia detonated an atomic weapon and it was revealed that the A-bomb secrets had been betrayed to Moscow. Panic followed, when even the Truman government was accused of harbouring Communist sympathisers and agents. America began to develop the hydrogen bomb – 'the destroyer of worlds' – a weapon equivalent in explosive power to 1,000 atomic bombs.

The first American H-bomb was exploded in 1954. Thereafter, the world has lived under the shadow of 'The Bomb', fearing sudden – even accidental – extinction.

New nations in South-East Asia

Japan's defeat in 1945 left South-East Asia in ferment. The European powers had claimed to be the protectors of their Asian subjects, yet their empires had fallen to the Japanese with ease, and their people endured harsh rule between 1942 and 1945. The age of imperialism had passed. In 1945, Japan had mischievously encouraged nationalist leaders in the Netherlands East Indies (Indonesia), Burma, Laos, Cambodia and the Vietnam states to declare their independence.

In 1945, British and Indian troops had landed in Indonesia and Indo-China to take the surrender of the Japanese forces there, maintaining order until the return of the Dutch and French. Australian troops were already in the Celebes and the Moluccas, but the Australian government refused to use them to quell local unrest and the troops were soon removed. In 1946, the United States gave the Philippines full independence, but the Dutch in Indonesia fought nationalist forces led by Achmed Sukarno, and the French troops in Indo-China were under attack by Ho Chi Minh's Viet Minh (Free Vietnam) fighters.

India, which had provided Britain with a volunteer army of two million men during the Second World War, was impatient for Britain to fulfil its pledge to grant it full independence. The new republics of India and Pakistan emerged in August 1947. Burma was granted independence from Britain in 1948, as was Ceylon (later named Sri Lanka). Britain's great south Asian empire had disappeared, but a new British Commonwealth was emerging.

The surrender of Japan, September 1945. Behind General MacArthur stand officers of the victorious powers (from left): China, Great Britain, Soviet Union, Australia (General Blamey), Canada, France, The Netherlands and New Zealand.

In 1948, Communist Chinese guerillas in Malaya began a terrorist campaign against the British. Most Western powers saw the unrest in South-East Asia as Communist inspired, but Australia's foreign policy was sympathetic to the independence movements, and often opposed British policy in the United Nations. Australia's Labor government led by Prime Minister Chifley supported Indonesia's demand for independence and welcomed the end of Dutch rule in Indonesia in 1949.

China

America was mostly concerned with events in China where, despite American military and monetary aid, Chiang Kai-shek's nationalist government was collapsing under pressure from Communist armies. In January 1949, Chiang fled from mainland China to the island of Formosa, and nationalist armies melted away before the advancing Communists. Mao Tse-tung established the People's Republic of China in Peiping on 1 October 1949. It seemed that the forward march of Communism could not be halted.

In the Australian federal election of December 1949, Chifley's Labor government faced a conservative coalition – the reborn Liberal Party under R. G. Menzies (who had lost office in 1941) in alliance with the Country Party. Menzies campaigned on a strong anti-Communist platform, warning of Communist influence in the trade unions and the growing **Red** menace in Asia. He promised to rebuild Australia's threadbare defence forces and reintroduce conscription. Menzies won by a landslide, and the Liberal Party were to remain in power until 1972.

Early in 1950, Australia signed the Colombo Plan agreement. In the agreement, developed nations in the British Commonwealth undertook to give aid and educational facilities to the undeveloped Commonwealth nations in an effort to reduce the appeal of Communism.

Japan

The Allied occupation of Japan was a success story. Under General MacArthur, the United States preserved the Emperor as a symbol of unity, introduced a new constitution, and set out to democratise Japan's closed society. Japan's reverence for authority made MacArthur's job easier. Australia provided the bulk of the forces in the British Commonwealth Occupation Force (BCOF) and an Australian judge presided over the trial that sentenced Japan's General Tojo to death for crimes against humanity. Other British, American, Australian and Dutch military tribunals sentenced nearly a thousand Japanese to death for war crimes.

Despite the birth of the UN, Australia was soon to enter several defence alliances with heavy obligations. These were combined with calls upon Australia to provide forces to fight aggressors, monitor cease-fires and protect victims of civil war as 'peace keepers' for the United Nations. Over the next half century, members of Australia's forces were to serve on two-thirds of UN peacekeeping missions – a proud record for any small nation. There would be hardly a year when elements of Australia's armed forces were not on duty somewhere in the world.

In June 1950, Menzies sent the first of two RAAF squadrons to Malaya to help the British. It was token of a new, active role in South-East Asia. One week later, Communist North Korean forces invaded South Korea. When the United Nations appealed to its members to help repel the aggressors, Australia responded immediately.

The new Indonesian Republic's leader President Sukarno (left), shown in the 1950s with India's Prime Minister Nehru.

1950: Korea: The Communist invasion

Korea, a remote land once known as the 'Hermit Kingdom', was an unlikely place to be the scene of the first war between Communism and the West. Japan annexed Korea in 1910 and sought to extinguish Korea's language and culture. On Japan's collapse in 1945, Russian armies invaded Manchuria and poured into Korea while American troops landed in the south. Both armies stopped at the 38th Parallel, which roughly divided Korea in half. In the north, a Communist 'People's Republic' was established under former guerilla leader Kim Il Sung, while in the south the Americans installed an émigré, Syngman Rhee, who was violently anti-Communist yet was also anti-**democratic**. Both leaders claimed to be the rightful rulers of Korea and vowed to unite the peninsula by force.

Australian infantrymen follow a British tank during the advancement to Korea's north late in 1950.

North Korea invades the South

North Korean armies invaded South Korea early on 25 June 1950, and quickly approached Seoul, the capital of the South. America assisted South Korea with supplies and ammunition and urged the United Nations to convene the Security Council. The Soviet representative had left the Council over a dispute several weeks before. He was unable to resume his seat in time to veto the Security Council's call on member nations to expel the North Korean aggressors. On 29 June 1950, North Korean tanks rolled into Seoul and the South Korean Army retreated to the south, accompanied by tens of thousands of refugees. On the next day, General MacArthur flew to the scene and informed President Truman that the only way of staving off disaster was to bring in American troops.

Britain and Australia were the first UN nations to offer support to the Americans. Several Australian naval vessels, an infantry battalion (3rd Battalion, Royal Australian Regiment) and a fighter squadron (77 Squadron, RAAF) were based in Japan. On 1 July, HMAS *Shoalhaven* sailed for Pusan. The next day, the RAAF were flying their Mustangs to escort US B-26 bombers in attacks on the Han bridges. On 26 July, Australia announced that the 3rd Battalion in Japan would also be sent to Korea, and called for volunteers to bring it to wartime strength of 1,000 men.

Fourteen other nations would later send combat forces to the United Nations command in Korea – Britain, New Zealand, Belgium, Canada, Colombia, Ethiopia, France, Greece, Luxembourg, the Netherlands, the Philippines, Thailand, Turkey and South Africa, while Denmark, India, Italy,

Norway and Sweden dispatched medical units. But the only troops immediately available to MacArthur, now named Commander-in-Chief of United Nations forces in Korea, was his under-strength army in Japan. Rushed into the front line, they were overwhelmed or forced into retreat.

In early August 1950, the long retreat halted behind the 200-kilometre line around the Pusan perimeter in the far south of Korea. There, UN supplies were stockpiled and US forces were concentrated along with reinforcements. Sensing that the North Korean advance had dangerously extended their forces, on 14 September MacArthur made a bold amphibious landing by US Marines on the west coast at Inchon, the port of Seoul, which forced the North Koreans into a headlong withdrawal from the South. On 29 September, MacArthur entered Seoul and requested approval to pursue the enemy north of the 38th Parallel. The Americans and South Koreans entered the North's capital of Pyongyang in mid-October.

American air attacks had eliminated North Korea's air force of Soviet-built Yaks and Stormoviks in the process. Soon, United Nations squadrons bombed enemy communications and troop concentrations.

By late September 1950, Australia's 3rd Battalion, RAR, joined British troops in Korea as part of the 'Commonwealth Brigade'. They spearheaded the Brigade's advance and by the end of October had almost reached the Yalu River, the border with Manchuria. Now American air forces were in combat against Chinese MiG jets based in Manchuria, which took a heavy toll until America's new Sabre jet arrived to meet them on equal terms. MacArthur predicted that the war would be over by Christmas. He was in for a nasty shock.

The Chinese offensive

On 26 November 1950, the Chinese launched their own offensive along the entire United Nations' front with 33 divisions, totalling 300,000 men. Rumours spread that 'the Chinese are in and the Third World War has begun!' The 8th Army, its right flank left open with the South Korean collapse, fell back.

By mid-December 1950, the United Nations' forces – accompanied by thousands of North Korean refugees – had retreated through the snows to a line below the 38th Parallel. The Commonwealth Brigade were the last troops to leave Seoul, which fell for the second time to Communist forces on 4 January 1951. The Australians were now on a new line, after a further 150-kilometre retreat. There, on 'Frostbite Ridge', they endured the bitter cold of January, cheered by the arrival of their fellow Anzacs – New Zealand's gunners.

Meteors were the first jet-fighters flown by Australian pilots, but they proved too slow to tackle the Communists' Russian-built MiG jets.

1951: Korea: Turning the tide

The Communist armies in Korea in 1951 totalled 400,000 men, the United Nations had only 200,000, but by mid-January the line was stabilised below the 38th Parallel and a UN counter-offensive began. When, in April, MacArthur stated that atomic weapons should be used, President Truman sacked him, replacing him as Commander-in-Chief with General Matthew B. Ridgway, the commander of 8th Army. MacArthur returned to the United States a popular hero and was urged to stand for president in the 1952 elections, but another general, Dwight Eisenhower, led the Republicans to victory, pledging to end the war in Korea.

In Australia, compulsory National Service of males began in 1951 (it lasted until 1959) and recruiting drives were mounted to increase the size of the forces in Korea.

The Battle of Kapyong

On 22 April 1951, nearly 60,000 Chinese infantry crossed the Imjin River under a massive artillery bombardment and fell on the United Nations' line. The Commonwealth Brigade, which was then in reserve, saw South Korean troops and their transports fleeing past its position in chaotic retreat. By 10 p.m. the Chinese bombardment was falling on the Australians who were defending Kapyong. To the sound of whistles and shouting, the Chinese charged in masses through point-blank Australian rifle and machine-gun fire. By dawn, the New Zealand gunners were deluging the attackers, but the Chinese continued and the Australians made a fighting withdrawal as night fell to link up with the British perimeter. By dawn on Anzac Day the attacks died off.

In June 1951, as the great Chinese offensive was held, the Soviet delegate to the UN called for a cease-fire and the re-establishment of the 38th Parallel as a separating line. The war was to last another two years. The dramatic advances and reverses of the first year settled into a long **stalemate**, as each side sought to gain another kilometre of ground on the ragged front line as 'bargaining power' at the peace table.

Australian soldiers carry a wounded American to safety during the fighting in Korea in 1951.

Australia's Prime Minister Menzies addresses the American Congress in Washington in 1950. Menzies believed that an American alliance was vital to Australia's security.

Stalemate in Korea

In October 1951, Australia's first aircraft carrier HMAS *Sydney* arrived in Korean waters for a difficult three-month tour of duty through a harsh winter. She carried two squadrons of Sea Furies – 805 and 808 Squadrons RAN, and 817 Squadron RAN, equipped with Fireflies. Operating off the east coast in appalling weather, and launching her aircraft by catapult, *Sydney* survived a typhoon and dispatched 2,700 strikes against North Korean targets in one month for the loss of nine aircraft.

While negotiations for an **armistice** continued, in July 1951 the United Kingdom and Commonwealth units were formed into the 1st British Commonwealth Division. The Division's first task – to cross the Imjin River and establish a 6,000-metre-deep bridgehead – was accomplished by September. In October 1951, the ground forces continued the struggle to seize the enemy-occupied heights on the Imjin Line.

The ANZUS Pact

In 1945, both Australia and New Zealand knew that their future security depended on American power, but the 'Anzac Pact' both countries signed with the United States in 1944 was little more than a deed of friendship.

Following Australia's prompt response to aid the United States in Korea, Australia's foreign minister Percy Spender began his successful attempt towards a formal defence alliance. America was receptive but made clear that it expected Australia and New Zealand to join her in signing a non-vindictive peace treaty with Japan. The ANZUS Pact was signed in September 1951, and Australia and New Zealand subsequently signed a peace treaty with Japan. Both treaties were approved by parliament in 1952.

ANZUS was a reward and consolation prize for Australia and New Zealand. In 1984, with the end of Communism as a threat and the disappearance of once-powerful Russian naval forces in the Pacific and Indian oceans, New Zealand ceased participating in ANZUS. But the pact with America – still known as ANZUS – remains the basis of Australia's defence policy, and Australian and New Zealand forces continue their close association in peace-keeping duties.

1953: Korea: Truce and aftermath

Political developments were bringing an end to the stalemated Korean War. In March 1953, Stalin died in Moscow and with him ended the worst of the terror of Communist rule. History would later reveal that under Stalin's rule 18 million of his people had been murdered or had died in labour camps. Stalin's successor Malenkov proposed a new policy of 'peaceful co-existence' with the West, and pressured Kim Il Sung to agree to an armistice. The Communists mounted a last series of offensives early in July 1953, but an armistice in Korea was signed on 27 July 1953. The ragged front line – which runs just north of the 38th Parallel – still serves as the border between the two Koreas.

The Korean War in retrospect

The Korean War was the first time that the West actively confronted Communism with armed force, but the cost was high. The war claimed the lives of 400,000 South Korean troops and more than 33,000 Americans. A total of 18,000 Australians had served in Korea, suffering 1,600 casualties including 293 dead; 37 New Zealanders died, part of the 3,000 dead suffered by non-American UN forces. Chinese and North Korean troops killed and wounded were estimated at 1.5 million. More than a million Korean civilians died.

The Korean War was described as a war between Communism and the forces of freedom, but South Korea knew little democratic freedom after the armistice. Under rule by the military after 1960, the country developed rapidly and its population grew to 44 million. In the 1990s, a democratically elected government took office.

The Korean War had been a boom period for Australia, where wool was bought by the Americans for their armed forces' uniforms at

Fifty years after the Korean War, the 38th Parallel still roughly marks the border between North and South Korea.

high prices; Japan's industries benefited from the demands for spare parts and vehicles.

In the 50 years since the war, North Korea went from bad to worse. By 1984, its economy was stagnant and some economic ties were initiated with South Korea. But the North remained a closed and repressive society under the rule of Kim Il Sung, who, after his death in 1995, was succeeded by his equally ruthless son Kim Jong Il. North Korea began a program to develop nuclear weapons while its people starved; one million died of hunger in the 1990s alone. The United States still regards the Marxist state as a threat to peace.

The 1950s: 'Thaw' ... and more war

As late as 1954, Australia's defence policy was oriented towards aiding the British to maintain their position in the Middle East. In that year, the two RAAF Vampire jet squadrons based in Malta were brought back to Australia. British forces left the Suez Canal Zone early in 1956 to concentrate their forces on Cyprus.

Early in 1956, the new Soviet leader Kruschev gave a speech to the Soviet Presidium revealing Stalin's crimes, and it seemed that the worst terrors of the Cold War were ending. But during 1956 uprisings in East Berlin, Poland and Hungary were crushed savagely by Russian tanks. At the same time the Middle East detonated. In July 1956, President Nasser of Egypt had seized control of the Suez Canal Company. Britain and France (the major shareholders) planned with Israel to invade Egypt and hopefully remove Nasser from power. The Commonwealth's senior statesman, Australia's Prime Minister Menzies, was asked to mediate the dispute but found Nasser immovable.

The Anglo-French-Israeli invasions of Egypt on 5 November 1956 appalled the United States. Britain was forced to order a cease-fire after two days. The war drove the Arab nations even further into the Soviet orbit. Australians have served with United Nations' units policing cease-fires in the Middle East since 1956.

By 1959, world tensions were easing. Britain and Australia abolished National Service. But soon new crises arose.

SEATO

Since 1946, the French had vainly fought to maintain their rule over Vietnam. But in May 1954, the great French fortress of Dien-Bien-Phu was captured after an epic siege by the Viet Minh and France admitted defeat. After the Geneva Conference, Vietnam was divided in two.

The United States soon created an alliance to combat the growth of Communist aggression – the South-East Asia Treaty Organization. Australia signed the SEATO pact in Manila in September 1954, along with America, Britain, France, the Philippines, Thailand, Pakistan and New Zealand.

SEATO was seen as an Asian counterpart to NATO, but soon proved a paper tiger. Unlike NATO, it had no integrated armed forces under a central command.

Far East Strategic Reserve

In April 1955, Australia's Prime Minister Menzies announced the creation of the 'British Commonwealth Strategic Reserve', an idea of the British. The force was to be based in Malaya and include British, New Zealand and Australian units. Soon an Australian battalion, four Australian warships and three RAAF squadrons would be based there.

The Malayan Emergency: Konfrontasi in Indonesia

In 1948, the British formed the Federation of Malaya in which the numerous Chinese inhabitants of Malaya were barely represented. This contributed to the violence unleashed by the Communist Chinese guerillas numbering 6,000 men who had fought bravely from their jungle hide-outs against the Japanese, but now sought to expel the British. Planters and officials were ambushed and killed, and Chinese communities were terrorised into giving support to the rebel groups who lived deep in the jungle and constantly outwitted the police. The 'Malayan Emergency' was to claim 12,000 lives over the next 12 years.

The Australian squadron's Lincoln bombers were to fly 4,000 sorties – mainly on bombing the terrorists' suspected jungle hide-outs – but succeeded in killing only 23 terrorists in eight years. This was a misguided strategy because the war was to be one of jungle patrols in search of an elusive enemy.

A new High Commissioner and Commander-in-Chief in Malaya, General Templer, arrived from London in 1952. He realized that there could be no military victory in Malaya without social and political reform. 'Tiger' Templer sacked the incompetent British authorities, and gained the confidence of the Malays and Chinese, encouraging them to sink their rivalries and form a single political party.

The Australian troops joined the 28th Commonwealth Brigade at Penang and began jungle operations against terrorists in January 1956. The terrorists, reduced in numbers and lacking support from the people, were driven into hiding. Malaya achieved independence in 1957, and the Malayan Emergency was declared over in 1960.

Australian soldiers served for years patrolling Malaysia's jungle borders with Indonesia.

Confrontation with Indonesia

In September 1963, the Federation of Malaysia was born, consisting of Malaya, Singapore and the Borneo territories of Sarawak and Sabah. Indonesia's President Sukarno vowed to crush Malaysia, a policy he called 'Konfrontasi' – confrontation. Sukarno saw Malaysia as both a threat and a rival.

Sukarno saw himself as a 'Third World' leader like Nehru of India and Tito of Yugoslavia, and vowed to end 'colonialism' which he described as a 'cancer in Asia'. Sukarno waged a successful diplomatic campaign (accompanied by border raids by the Indonesian military) to expel the Dutch from western New Guinea – West Irian. The territory was awarded to Indonesia by the United Nations in 1963, despite the fact that the native inhabitants – Melanesians – had a culture alien to anything found in Indonesia.

Indonesia, which is more than 80 per cent Muslim and rich in natural resources, is an island nation of more than 500 dialects. Its unity has always been fragile, and many of its people resent the harsh rule from Java. Sukarno's domestic and foreign policy was a juggling act.

In December 1963, Indonesian troops mounted a raid on a border post in Sabah, killing eight Malaysians. In August 1964, the Indonesians landed a small force on the coast of Johore, and in the following month paratroopers were dropped. All the infiltrators were rounded up, but Indonesian raids continued, and Australia joined New Zealand in promising support to Malaysian and British forces in resisting aggression.

Australian defences grow, 1964

In November 1964, Prime Minister Menzies announced a massive increase in Australia's defence spending. The strength of the Regular Army would be increased 50 per cent over three years from 22,000 effectives to 33,000, providing for a full three-brigade division of nine battalions. RAAF and RAN personnel would be increased by about 25 per cent. New aircraft would be purchased – Mirage fighters, American F-111 strike aircraft, modernised Hercules transports, long endurance Orion maritime reconnaissance aircraft, and Italian Macchi trainers. To provide the additional personnel, conscription would be introduced – from numbers chosen by lottery from a register of 20-year-old males. Failure to register would be an offence. To most Australians, Indonesia was seen as a major threat to security, and the possibility of outright war was openly discussed.

In February 1965, the crack multi-purpose commando unit, 1st Special Air Service Squadron (SAS) – 100 officers and men – arrived in Brunei.

Above: Australian and Malaysian officers discuss a patrol.

And in March, 3 RAR deployed in Sarawak, joining British and Gurkha units in more than 30 strikes across the borders.

The fall of Sukarno, 1965

Confrontation ended suddenly. On 30 September 1965, a small number of Indonesian army and air force officers in Jakarta, possibly aided by Communists close to Sukarno, attempted to seize power. The army under General Suharto crushed the coup and a backlash against suspected Communist sympathisers was led by army units and Muslim extremists. Within a few years, more than 500,000 Indonesians who were suspected of Communist sympathies were killed, with others thrown into prison. Suharto sought to repair relations with the West in return for financial and military assistance, and called an end to confrontation. Suharto became Indonesia's president in 1967 and remained in power until 1998, when Indonesia's economy collapsed and his corruption was revealed. The turbulent but charismatic Sukarno died in 1970, but his daughter Megawati Sukarnoputri became President of the Republic in 2001.

Vietnam: Nationalism and Communism

The French defeat

In 1965, just as conflict with Indonesia was averted, Vietnam became the scene of another 'bushfire war'. It became a more terrible conflict than the Korean War.

In July 1945, the Allied powers meeting in Berlin had decided that after Japan's surrender Indo-China would be returned to French control. Vietnam (Cochin China, Tonkin and Annam) would be occupied temporarily by Chinese forces in the north, and British forces in the south, with the 16th Parallel forming the dividing line. The French returned later in 1945 to find that the Vietnamese leader Ho Chi Minh, a Communist, had already proclaimed independence.

After all attempts to find a political solution failed, Ho's Viet Minh (Free Vietnam) Army attacked the French in Hanoi and Saigon in December 1946. It was the beginning of a savage war that would continue for nearly 30 years. The French were unused to jungle warfare and their forces suffered heavy casualties. The United States provided finance and military equipment to support the French in Indo-China. President Eisenhower described the countries of South-East Asia as 'dominoes' and stated that if one fell to Communism the others would surely follow.

Early in 1954, the French decided to construct a huge base in Vietnam's north in a valley called Dien Bien Phu from where they could mount operations against the elusive Viet Minh. The base became their tomb. The enemy hauled guns up to the mountains surrounding it, besieging its **garrison** of 30,000 French and Colonial troops. After a heroic two-month defence, the fortress of Dien Bien Phu surrendered in May 1954. It was the end of France's rule in Indo-China.

The resulting Geneva Protocols established the independent monarchies of Laos and Cambodia, while Vietnam – the Communist-ruled North and the Western-supported South – was to be divided by the 17th Parallel, separated by a demilitarised zone (DMZ). The two halves, each consisting of about 15 million people, were to be united following elections to be held in 1956, the year when the last French forces would leave.

America steps in, 1962

No elections were held in 1956, and Communist Viet Cong guerillas soon attempted to overthrow the government in South Vietnam. They ambushed officials and village leaders and soon dominated vast areas of the South. President Kennedy, who became US President early in 1961, decided to play a more active role in resisting the Communist guerillas. In 1962, an army of 10,000 American military advisers helped train the Army of the Republic of Vietnam (ARVN) in counter-insurgency.

In that year, American Intelligence reported that the Saigon government had control of barely 40 per cent of the country; that the mass of the peasants – many of whom were terrified of Viet Cong retribution – had no confidence in Diem's government; that few roads were safe; and that provincial army chiefs in the South were incompetent or corrupt. It was hardly a firm base on which to build the greatest armed American counter-offensive against Communism since Korea.

Australian advisers in Vietnam

The Australian government viewed the situation with concern, and in May 1962 sent a small force of 32 Australian jungle warfare experts to South Vietnam. The Australian Army Training Team Vietnam (AATTV) – known as the 'Team' – was to serve for 10 years in Vietnam, total 222 personnel and become the most highly decorated unit in Australian history, winning four Victoria Crosses and hundreds of other medals and citations for bravery.

By 1964, sizeable units of the North Vietnamese Army (NVA) were infiltrating the South to support the Viet Cong, and the Saigon government seemed to be tottering. A White House report stated that 'South Vietnam is regarded as a test case of US capacity to help a nation meet a Communist "war of liberation".'

At a SEATO conference in Manila, America asked member nations to provide military assistance to the South Vietnamese, but only Australia agreed; the size of the Advisory Team was doubled. Five months later, in August 1964, RAAF Caribou transports arrived at Vung Tau airfield near Saigon to help the Americans.

The *Voyager* tragedy

In night exercises off the southern coast of New South Wales in February 1964, the destroyer *Voyager* steamed across the bows of the aircraft carrier HMAS *Melbourne*, and was cut in two, sinking with the tragic loss of 82 men including her captain. In 1969, an American destroyer also collided with *Melbourne* and sank. In both cases, the captains of the carrier were transferred to a shore posting – equivalent to disciplinary action – and they promptly resigned. Australians were outraged by the Navy's willingness to find scapegoats.

Left: Australian forces thought that new tactics could defeat the Communists in Vietnam. Here, Australian troops are air-lifted into action.

Below: Australia's aircraft-carrier HMAS *Melbourne* saw an enormous range of service in South-East Asian waters for nearly 30 years, but is chiefly remembered for her collision with the destroyer HMAS *Voyager*.

1965-66: Vietnam: The war widens

On 7 August 1964, after what he described as 'attacks' by North Vietnamese forces on the US Navy ships on patrol in the Gulf of Tonkin, President Johnson was granted by Congress authority to pursue the war in Vietnam. He ordered bombing attacks on North Vietnam. More Americans were killed in Viet Cong terrorist attacks, and American anger mounted.

Below: The enemy proved elusive for American troops in Vietnam.

'Escalation' begins

In March 1965, President Johnson began a three-month bombing offensive – 'Rolling Thunder' – against North Vietnam. In April, the new American commander in Vietnam, General Westmoreland, suggested that Australia be asked to contribute a battalion. In June 1965, Johnson announced that American forces would be increased to 125,000 by the end of the year. In response, North Vietnam began infiltrating more troops into the South along the 'Ho Chi Minh trail' on the mountainous western borders. Escalation had begun and there was no turning back.

By the end of 1965, American ground forces in South Vietnam numbered 200,000 and within two years were to reach their peak of 550,000, while South Vietnam's army was to total 700,000. But among Johnson's closest advisers, many were soon questioning the wisdom of escalation and whether the war was winnable under any conditions.

Australian forces committed

On 29 April 1965, only four days after the 50th anniversary of the Gallipoli landings, Prime Minister Menzies announced that Australia was dispatching an infantry battalion to Vietnam. Many Australians were distressed by the government's decision to send young conscripts to Vietnam in 1966. More than 15,000 young men were to serve in Vietnam and suffer half the total Australian casualties. Menzies resigned in January 1966, leaving his successor Harold Holt to endure increasing criticism of Australian involvement in the conflict.

First actions

In May 1965, 1st Battalion Royal Australian Regiment arrived by air at the American base at Bien Hoa. They had been trained in jungle conditions in Queensland and were to prove fine and skilled soldiers.

It was a new kind of war. There was no front line. The enemy was rarely seen. Mines were to account for half of Australia's 3,000 casualties.

By mid-1966, 1st Australian Task Force was formed and deployed in Phuoc Tuy province, south-east of Saigon. The province was dominated by the Viet Cong and the vital road – Route 15 – between the capital and the port of Vung Tau was under constant attack. Viet Cong and North Vietnamese forces were known to number at least 6,000 men. From its new base at Nui Dat, the Task Force began major operations to clear the enemy. The Australians soon came under scattered fire, and the first young conscript was killed during these operations.

The Battle of Long Tan, 1966

Ambushes were a constant threat. In August 1966, the Australians walked into one and it became their biggest battle in Vietnam.

After the Australian base at Nui Dat was hit by mortar fire on the night of 16–17 August 1966, a company of 6th Battalion was sent out the next day on a 'search and destroy' mission. The Australians made their way across the paddy-fields in steaming heat, past the village of Long Tan, which was a known Viet Cong centre. Waiting to ambush the 100 Australians was a force of 2,500 Viet Cong and North Vietnamese regulars.

The main body of Australians moving into the rubber plantation were suddenly hit by a deluge of mortar shells and small arms fire. As pouring rain came down, the Australians immediately formed a perimeter, scratched weapon-pits out of the mud and fought back wave after wave of attackers.

In the furious three-hour battle, 18 Australians were killed, 24 wounded; the dead bodies of 245 Viet Cong were found. Intelligence estimated that as many as 350 enemy soldiers had been wounded and dragged away. The Australians had been outnumbered 20 to one, and had fought in nightmare conditions of rain and mud.

During 1967, the Australians secured Phuoc Tuy province which became the base of the biggest force of Australians since the Second World War, totalling four battalions. Three RAAF squadrons were in Vietnam – 35 Squadron flying Caribou transports; 2 Squadron flying Canberra jet bombers and the famed 9 Squadron flying Iroquois helicopters (fitted with machine-guns, these were called the 'Bushrangers'). The RAN was also present – the carrier *Sydney* carried the troops and equipment, and *Perth*, *Hobart*, *Brisbane*, and *Vendetta* all saw service in Vietnam waters.

Left: Australians tending to their wounded after the Battle of Long Tan in 1966.

1968-72:
Vietnam: The war runs down

The Tet offensive

Early in 1968, the American commanders were predicting that victory in Vietnam was just around the corner. But in February, the Viet Cong struck with a savagery that showed they were unbeaten. Enemy cadres infiltrated Saigon and entered the grounds of the US Embassy, and others seized the city of Hue. The Americans retook it, but destroyed the city in the process.

The Tet offensive was stemmed and the enemy lost close to 100,000 men, but America's cause was damaged. Demonstrations protesting against the war crowded the cities of the world.

In March 1968, when Westmoreland asked for another 250,000 men, Johnson announced that he was not seeking re-election to the presidency. The failed war had broken him. The bombing of North Vietnam was halted and the first moves were made to hold peace talks. But in May, the North Vietnamese launched another offensive: Australian troops fought back enemy attacks for three weeks of intense fighting.

Withdrawal

In 1968, Richard Nixon had been elected US president vowing to end the Vietnam War, but he too proved unwilling to admit defeat. In May 1970, Nixon ordered American and ARVN forces

Left: Australian infantry accompanied by Centurion tanks enter a Vietnamese village in search of Viet Cong in 1969.

into Cambodia to clear the Viet Cong sanctuaries there and cut the enemy's supply route along the Ho Chi Minh trail. The invasion served only to destabilise Cambodia.

American forces were gradually reduced as they handed over military and civil duties to South Vietnamese units.

Conscription

In Australia, the early protests against young conscripts being sent to Vietnam (such as the 'Save Our Sons' demonstrators) grew into a nationwide anger against Australia's involvement in 'an immoral war'.

On 8 May 1970, mass demonstrations by more than 120,000 people took place in Australian cities – the first of the **moratoriums**. The Labor Party spoke out increasingly against the immorality of the war. In September, 50,000 people marched in Melbourne alone. Slowly, the Australian and American forces in Vietnam were reduced, but the troops returned home without victory parades. Public opinion was now against the war and wanted it ended. The troops, who had done their duty, were the scapegoats of a war made by politicians.

By 1972, American ground forces had been reduced to 50,000 men. In December 1972, Labor governments swept into power in both New Zealand and Australia. The new Australian Prime Minister Gough Whitlam announced the cessation of military aid to South Vietnam, and the withdrawal of all remaining Australian personnel.

The cease-fire was signed in Paris in January 1973. In South Vietnam, the situation deteriorated rapidly. The North Vietnamese Army launched a sudden, overwhelming offensive with 27 divisions in April 1975, and entered Saigon on 30 April 1975, finally uniting Vietnam.

Nearly 50,000 Australians had served in Vietnam and they suffered 501 fatalities. The wounded numbered 2,400. National Servicemen had suffered 43 per cent of all Australian casualties.

The war left 56,000 Americans dead, 303,000 wounded and a debt (after 1965) of US$109,000 million – destroying America's unchallenged economic domination of the world. South Vietnamese casualties were 185,000 dead and 500,000 wounded. Viet Cong and North Vietnamese killed in action numbered 937,000 while civilian dead totalled 415,000 with 915,000 wounded. Twenty years after the end of the war, the Vietnamese government claimed that three million Vietnamese died, but Vietnam, still Communist-ruled, seems purged of hate. It is a relatively peaceful society that has opened its doors to Western investment and tourism. Today, Australian visitors wonder how only 30 years ago a war could have been waged with such savagery.

The Vietnam War had a bitter legacy. A large number of Australians felt it a disgrace. Opposition was so great that units mounted no marches to mark their return from war. Soldiers later reported strange illnesses that were traceable to the poisonous defoliant – Agent Orange – sprayed by Americans widely. For a generation, the 50,000 Australian veterans formed a 'forgotten army'.

Cambodia falls, 1975

In the same month as the fall of Saigon, the Marxist forces – the Khmer Rouge (Red Cambodia) – led by Pol Pot took power in Cambodia. The Vietnam War was over, but more than two million Cambodians were to die under pitiless Khmer Rouge rule before Vietnamese forces invaded Cambodia in 1978, driving Pol Pot into a jungle refuge on the Thai border. Australian soldiers would later oversee the return of an elected government to Cambodia in 1993, but until then the Cambodians suffered horrifically.

Indonesians enter Timor, 1975

When it seemed that Marxist groups were likely to achieve power in newly independent East Timor, Indonesian troops entered the former Portuguese colony in November 1975. There was no protest from America. A week later, Australia underwent its own 'coup' when the Governor-General sacked the Labor government, and Timor's tragedy was soon forgotten.

The 1970s: A decade of change

After the Vietnam experience, Australians turned their back on the world's problems. The Labor government led by Gough Whitlam (1972–75) was determined to reform Australian society rather than commit forces to the world's trouble spots. The 1970s saw endless fighting between Israel and the Palestine Liberation Organization (PLO), and civil wars broke-out in the former Portuguese **colonies** in Africa where each side was supplied with arms by the Soviet Union or the West.

Early in 1972, Gough Whitlam had been a visitor to Communist China, with which he hoped to establish a closer relationship. Later in 1972, President Nixon, who had campaigned for 25 years on a hard-line anti-Communist program, visited China to normalise Sino-American relations, ending the West's quarantine of Red China. China now took the seat in the UN Security Council previously held by Taiwan. It was a sign of the changing times that SEATO

During the 1970s and 1980s, Australia withdrew into herself. Still smarting from the defeat in Vietnam, she provided few forces for the UN peace-keeping duties.

was dissolved in 1977. Sponsored by the United States and the European powers, it was now irrelevant in the new Asia.

Asia was to experience an unusual period of stability, darkened only by the killings in Cambodia. The focus of unrest was shifting once more to the Middle East. Conflict between Arabs and Jews had led to another war in 1973, and Israel was nearly defeated. In that year, the Arab oil-producing nations took independent action against the West by doubling and then tripling oil prices, forcing the West into **recession**.

In 1973, Britain entered the European Common Market – later the European Union, finally ending her role as an imperial power.

The American bases

The American alliance was strengthened by Australia permitting the US to establish top-secret communications bases on her territory. The base at North-West Cape opened in 1967, Pine Gap near Alice Springs opened in 1968, and Nurrungar north-west of Adelaide opened in 1971. These valuable, jointly administered listening posts and satellite monitoring stations are a key element in America's 'eyes and ears' in the southern hemisphere.

The bases indicated a new step in warfare. Much of the data was received from satellites. In the 1980s, digitised systems revolutionised weaponry.

Australian Defence Force (ADF) born, 1976

In 1973, the Labor government combined the five defence ministries (Defence, Navy, Army, Air Force and Supply) into a single Department of Defence. In 1975, it went further and brought together the three armed services as the Australian Defence Force (ADF) under a central commander – the Chief of Defence Force – for the first time in their history. The ADF's birth was officially 1 January 1976, and it was divided into Maritime (Navy), Land (Army) and Air (RAAF) Commands, and Northern Command in Darwin. The ADF's headquarters are in Canberra.

This small, all-volunteer, highly trained defence force was to carry out two roles with remarkable ability: defending Australia's shores while serving wherever it was needed – mostly under the United Nations. The Liberal Fraser government had made cuts in defence spending in 1977, but bolstered expenditure in 1980, enabling two locally built FFG-7 guided-missile frigates to join the four being bought from the United States. The flotilla consists of HM Australian Ships *Adelaide*, *Sydney*, *Canberra*, *Darwin*, *Newcastle* and *Torrens*. In 1981, Australia ordered 75 new F/A-18 (Hornet) fighter aircraft to replace the ageing Mirage 111s. Twenty-two years later, the Hornets saw their first active service in Iraq.

Women in the armed forces

In 1985, women were admitted to the Navy, Army and Air Force on the same basis as men and the separate women's services such as the WRAAF and the WRANS were dissolved. Women now underwent weapons training in combat conditions alongside men, though they were still barred from combat positions in the infantry, tanks (armour) and combat squadrons of the Air Force.

Soon, Australia had female pilots flying transport planes, and serving on duties ranging from signallers and mechanics to military police. By the 2003 Iraq War, one-sixth of America's armed forces were female, and female sailors comprised 20 per cent of the ship's company of HMAS *Kanimbla* on active service in the Persian Gulf.

The Cold War ends, new wars begin

The end of the Cold War

By the mid-1980s, the Communist bloc was almost bankrupt. Its leaders could hold out few promises of a better life to their people. In 1986, Premier Gorbachev, the architect of a new freedom in the Soviet Union ('Glasnost'), met with American President Reagan, and proposed an end to the arms race. It was the beginning of the end of the Cold War.

Three years later came the collapse of the Communist bloc in Europe. In late 1989, the people of eastern Europe took to the streets and demanded freedom and democracy. Soviet troops had mostly been withdrawn and their own armed forces stood to one side, even when Berliners began demolishing the **Berlin Wall**. The revolution was almost bloodless.

A new defence policy

The new Australian Labor government in 1983 had to determine what role the defence forces would play in the new world scene. In 1982, the last aircraft carrier, HMAS *Melbourne*, had been decommissioned and plans were made to buy the Royal Navy's carrier *Invincible,* but the latter was used in the campaign later that year to recapture the Falkland Islands from Argentina, and Britain decided to keep it.

The Hawke government's Dibb Report of 1986 stated that Australia no longer faced immediate external threats. The report recommended concentrating on developing systems of detecting and intercepting intruders by both conventional means (i.e. the purchase of six patrol vessels) and electronic means (over-the-horizon radar, airborne early warning aircraft and electronic sensors). In the 1990s, the focus of Australia's defence moved to the north of the continent.

The end of Anzac?

In 1984, New Zealand, which had proclaimed a 'Nuclear Free Zone' in the Pacific and sent a frigate into the French atomic test zone to protest on behalf of the people of the Pacific islands, withdrew from ANZUS. This was a result of her refusal to admit American nuclear-powered and armed warships to her harbours for the 1985 ANZUS exercises.

New Zealand's remote geographical position gives her a security that Australia lacks. She has always looked towards the Pacific while Australia has looked anxiously towards Asia. New Zealand has reduced her armed forces to a bare minimum (scrapping her fighter wing) while Australia is planning to replace both her ageing Hornet fighters and F-111 fighter-bombers (strike aircraft) with modern types. Many New Zealanders have accused their own government of unfairly relying on Australia to shoulder the main burden of regional defence.

The challenges of a 'super power'

America's victory in the Cold War was in many ways a hollow one. Economically, the cost had been high. America's dominance in technology, however, was unchallenged. As national boundaries blurred in the growth of '**globalisation**', America faced new economic challenges from the

European Economic Community (soon to be the European Union) and the rapidly developing economies in South-East Asia. It also soon faced a military and ideological threat from a newly emerging power, militant Islam.

Iraq and the Gulf War, 1991

The overthrow in January 1979 of the corrupt Pahlevi dynasty in Iran by its fundamentalist anti-Western Islamic opposition, and the Soviet invasion of Afghanistan in December 1979 devastated the stability of the Middle East. The rise to power of Saddam Hussein in Iraq in the same year was also devastating to the region.

Supplied with Western arms, the Afghan *mujahedeen* fought a 10-year guerilla war against the Russians, who lost 15,000 men killed, before withdrawing from Afghanistan in 1989. They left a way open for a ruthless fundamentalist minority, the Taliban, to take power over Afghanistan.

The West had supported Saddam Hussein's Iraq with arms and Saudi Arabia and Kuwait had assisted it with subsidies in Iraq's long war with Iran (1980–88), only to find that Saddam's regime was far more unpredictable and ruthless than Iran's. Stalemated by Iran's superior resources and manpower, Saddam Hussein turned his attentions to an easier prey, one whose existence Iraq had always questioned – the tiny, oil-rich kingdom of Kuwait. In August 1990, Iraqi forces invaded Kuwait.

The United Nations, recognising the grave threat to the region's peace and the world's oil supplies, immediately called for the withdrawal of Iraqi forces. On 26 August 1990, the UN requested members to provide warships to enforce a maritime blockade of Iraq. The Australian warships *Adelaide*, *Darwin*, *Sydney*, *Brisbane*, *Supply*, *Success* and *Westralia* were all to serve in the Persian Gulf multi-national fleet in the first year of the Gulf War; and Australian warships are still on patrol there.

On 24 February 1991, the United Nations ground offensive began with American, British, French, Syrian and Egyptian tanks following American night-fighting rocket-equipped Apache attack helicopters, completely destroying the Iraqi defences in Kuwait in three days. It had been the quickest and most devastating victory in military history. Saddam Hussein remained in power during the 1990s, but Iraq's hapless people suffered the consequences of his aggression in crippling UN sanctions.

Left: When Australian forces were sent overseas to join the coalition against Iraq, many Australians mounted mass protests against the government's decision.

Australia's armed forces – the Australian Defence Force (ADF) – were modernized in the early 1980s. This photograph shows a Mirage fighter (top) and its replacement, an F/A-18 Hornet fighter, which is still in operation.

Peace keeping for the United Nations

In other regions wracked by the consequences of war and **genocide**, solutions were equally difficult. In May 1991, a form of peace finally came to Cambodia when the four warring factions – including the remnants of the Khmer Rouge, who had killed nearly one-third of the population – agreed to hold elections supervised by the United Nations. During 1992, the United Nations Transitional Authority in Cambodia grew to a force of 22,000 (including more than 500 Australians) under the command of an Australian, Lieutenant-General John Sanderson. Elections were held in May 1993, and Cambodia once more became a monarchy under Sihanouk in uneasy alliance with a former Khmer Rouge functionary, Hun Sen, as Prime Minister.

A large Australian force served in Somalia where United Nations forces arrived in 1992 to avert the collapse of the country by famine at the hands of warlords. In January 1993, 1st Battalion RAR and supporting units (comprising nearly 1,000 troops in all) were posted to Somalia. They returned, mission accomplished, in May.

Modern armed forces

In the late 1990s, the Australian Defence Force was a small but highly trained all-volunteer force of professionals whose effectiveness would soon be tested. Land Command (Army) consisted of close to 30,000 men and women, organised into four brigades (one at Townsville, two at Brisbane and a fourth at Sydney) with armour (Leopard tanks), artillery, engineers and support services. The 3rd Brigade formed the Operational Deployment force. The strength of the Air Command (RAAF) lay in its three tactical fighter squadrons (flying F/A-18s), two strike/reconnaissance squadrons (flying F-111s), two maritime patrol squadrons (flying Orions) and five transport squadrons.

By late 2001, only one destroyer, HMAS *Brisbane*, remained in commission in the RAN. But the government planned to buy three new destroyers. The Navy's strength lay in its six FFG frigates (*Adelaide*, *Canberra*, *Sydney*, *Darwin*, *Melbourne* and *Newcastle*) and its three new Anzac-class patrol frigates, the first of which, HMAS *Anzac*, joined the fleet in 1996. The first of six planned Australian-built submarines HMAS *Collins*, was also launched in 1996, and between 1998 and 2001 five more were commissioned – *Farncomb*, *Waller*, *Dechaineux*, *Sheean* and *Rankin*.

Lieutenant-General John Sanderson commanded the UN force in Cambodia.

Top right: Two Australian soldiers wearing the blue caps of the United Nations in Cambodia.

Bottom right: An Indonesian soldier guards the front of a military transport truck carrying Australian troops into Dili, East Timor, on 20 September 1999.

Australia's anxieties are now fixed on the 'Near North', near where the bulk of her land forces are based – not to face invasion by foreign armies, but ready for rapid deployment in battalion or brigade strength where and when they are needed.

Timor

As a century of war ended, Australian forces were next deployed on an island that had long links with Australia. Australians were aware of the part played by the people of East Timor in helping their soldiers in the dark days of 1942–43. They watched with unease Indonesia's attempts after 1975 to obliterate East Timor's unique identity. As repression of the East Timorese intensified, a national unease became anger and then disgust at the Australian government's inactivity. When Australia sent in troops at the request of the United Nations to bring an end to the oppression, the nation cheered.

In May 1998, following widespread economic collapse in South-East Asian nations that left Indonesia's economy in tatters, a breakdown of law in her scattered territories and massed street riots in Jakarta forced the resignation of Indonesian President Suharto. International pressure grew on Indonesia's new President Habibie to resolve the East Timor problem. In January 1999, Habibie offered the province a 'new status'. Within two weeks, Australia had offered to provide troops for a UN peace-keeping force. UN teams, arriving in Dili in March to begin preparations for the voting, reported increasing violence by the Indonesian military and the Jakarta-sponsored 'militias'.

Into East Timor, 1999

The UN was thus fully forewarned of the tragic events that followed East Timor's 30 August ballot, which saw a majority vote for independence. The people's joy was short-lived. Within hours, the machete-wielding militias went on a rampage of killing, burning and kidnapping.

On 9 September 1999, Habibie announced Indonesia's agreement to the presence of an international force in East Timor. On 15 September 1999, the UN Security Council authorised a multinational force to use 'all necessary means' to restore order: the International Force East Timor (INTERFET) would consist of 8,000 personnel, to which Australia would contribute the largest number (4,500). It would be commanded by an Australian, Major-General Peter Cosgrove, and the first Australian troops would be provided by 3rd Brigade at Darwin.

On 20 September 1999, elements of the 2nd Battalion, Royal Australian Regiment, landed from aircraft at Dili airport and quickly fanned out to secure it. It was the prelude to a massive airlift of troops, transport, supplies and food. The Australians re-occupied East Timor within a month. Between 1 and 23 February 2000, INTERFET handed over control in East Timor to UNTAET (United Nations Transitional Authority East Timor), now comprised of units from 23 nations wearing the blue cap. But 2,000 Australian personnel stayed behind.

Islam and the West

September 11, 2001

On the morning of 11 September 2001, a terrifying event shocked the world. Islamic extremists hijacked four American airliners and crashed two of them into the symbol of the United States' financial might – the twin towers of the World Trade Center in New York. A third plane crashed into the Pentagon in Washington. These terrorist acts resulted in the death of nearly 3,000 people, among them more than 20 Australians. President George W. Bush described the attacks as acts of war against the United States. Bush vowed retaliation against global terrorism, pledging to bring to justice those responsible for the attack, and to punish all who harboured and encouraged them.

The suspected mastermind of the attack was a fanatic, Osama (or Usama) bin Laden. Born into a millionaire Saudi family, he had funded attacks on American embassies and properties, and had been forced to seek refuge in Taliban-ruled Afghanistan, where his activities were encouraged.

Afghanistan

When the Taliban refused American requests to hand over Osama bin Laden, United States and British aircraft and missiles were launched in October 2001 against Afghanistan, striking suspected guerrilla camps and Taliban communications sites as prelude to a ground campaign to end Taliban rule.

Assisted by constant American bombing and missile attacks on Taliban headquarters, airfields and bases, the Northern Alliance forces – adequately equipped with tanks and weaponry – rapidly struck south, and by mid-November 2001 entered Kabul, driving the broken Taliban across the Pakistan border. In captured Kandahar, Western intelligence officers found evidence that the September 11 fanatics and the fugitive Osama bin Laden were members of a worldwide Islamic terrorist network – the al Q'aeda – which was planning continuous attacks on a number of Western and Western-aligned countries.

The Bush doctrine: 'Zero tolerance'

In his first State of the Union address (January 2002), President George W. Bush named Iraq, Iran and North Korea as training grounds for Islamic extremists, part of an 'axis of evil' seeking to hold the world to ransom. The United States informed the UN that Saddam Hussein was harbouring Islamic extremist terrorist groups and developing nuclear, biological and chemical warfare – 'Weapons of Mass Destruction' (WMDs). It was impossible to verify the latter claim as Saddam Hussein had expelled the UN

Left: An undated photograph of Iraqi leader Saddam Hussein, who 'disappeared' with the fall of his regime on 9 April, 2003.

weapons inspectors in 1998. Iraq's regime was nearing collapse. The UN seized its oil revenues to pay for food for the Iraqi people, while Saddam and his family continued to live like kings.

In March 2003, President Bush attempted to obtain a resolution from the UN Security Council that Iraq disarm or face armed invasion, but France and Russia announced they would veto such a resolution and stated that further negotiation was necessary. By this date, the United States had gathered an armed force of 350,000 personnel (army, airmen and navy) in the Gulf region, along with forces from the only nations that had promised to support an American action against Iraq – Britain and Australia.

Britain sent to the Gulf a third of her army – more than 30,000 troops. Australia dispatched a total of three warships, a squadron of fourteen F/A18 (Hornet) jet fighters and Orion and Hercules aircraft, in addition to the crack SAS unit and Commandos from 4RAR: a total of 2,000 personnel. On 18 March 2003, President Bush issued an ultimatum to Hussein to leave his country within 48 hours or face the consequences. On its expiry, American missiles and air attacks were launched against Baghdad.

On 21 March, American and British tanks entered Iraq from Kuwait. An American armoured-column raced for Baghdad and the British landed near Basra, while the air-attack on Iraqi military and communications positions – and Saddam's palaces – continued, with very few civilian casualties. Within a week, Iraqi resistance was stiffening and the Americans intensified their air attacks. The American tanks pressed on and by Day 14 they had seized Baghdad airport. During the third week of war, American tanks were in the streets of Baghdad. Saddam Hussein had disappeared and his government fled. The Americans had suffered 100 battle fatalities, the British half that number. Australian Special Forces and Hornet fighters had been in action since the first day but suffered no casualties.

To achieve quick victory, the Americans had resorted to a massive use of airpower and missiles, which destroyed Iraq's **infrastructure**. After six months, Allied forces had found no evidence of chemical or nuclear weaponry in mid-July 2003. The new Iraqi provisional government declared 9 April (the day when Saddam Hussein disappeared and Baghdad fell) as the day of liberation. America has appealed to other nations to provide forces to help maintain order while she undertakes the rebuilding of the country.

Below: Chief of the Australian Defence Force, General Peter Cosgrove, surveys US aerial damage to a presidential palace on the outskirts of Baghdad, 27 April, 2003.

Defending Australia

The faithful ally

A close alliance with the United States is the basis of Australia's defence policy. Few voices are raised for a policy of **neutralism**. Asia's rapid economic development is seen as beneficial, not threatening, and concerns in the 20th century about Asia's millions invading Australia's deserts are now seen as alarmist nonsense.

Fear of Asian Communism has been replaced by anxiety about Indonesia's instability. Of the Indonesian Republic's 200 million people, 87 per cent are Muslims, most of whom belong to the peaceable Sunni faith and have no feelings of hostility to Australia. Islamic terrorism is rising, and more than 100 Australians have been killed in two terrorist attacks in New York and Bali. Many Australians felt their government was overreacting and displaying callousness when boatloads of Iraqi, Iranian and Afghan refugees heading from Indonesian ports for Australia's northern coast were turned back or detained in camps. They were fleeing oppressive regimes, but the Howard government pointed out that many were being smuggled in by organised crime who profited by their suffering. Following the restoration of Australia's links with Indonesia, police have now taken action against the 'people smugglers'.

Terrorist threats

Unless a peaceful solution can be found, the West lives under the threat of terrorist attacks by Islamic extremists consumed with hatred for the West and for past wrongs. Extremists have already made attempts to bring down the world's computer systems through assaults on the Internet – cyber warfare. All people dread terrorist use of chemical or biological weapons or even primitive nuclear bombs against America and its allies. It is clear that if further attacks are made on American cities or citizens, America will continue to retaliate.

An Australian soldier carries logs of ice at the base in Baghdad, Iraq, July 2003. Australia has sent 2000 personnel to join the coalition forces during the fall of Saddam Hussein's regime.

Peace keepers

The unsung heroes of the United Nations are the small groups of military personnel who volunteer for lonely duty in danger spots in remote areas of the world. The British Commonwealth has provided an enormous number of personnel to serve as observers (many of them unarmed) and in units separating warring factions. Australians have policed the truce in Kashmir (1950–85); served often in Sinai and on the Lebanese border; helped bring about the truce in Yemen (1963); maintained RAAF helicopter patrols in the Sinai (1976–1993); and served as peace keepers at the birth of Zimbabwe (1979) and Namibia (1989); in addition to seeing service from Rwanda to Somalia.

Pacific police

Closer to home, Australia has assumed responsibilities with New Zealand to provide forces to restore stability in Pacific nations facing internal collapse. In 2003, when the Australian Peace Monitoring group returned from long duty in Bougainville (the rebellious island has achieved autonomy from Papua New Guinea rule), a large Australian force began landing on Guadalcanal in the southern Solomons. Its duty is to protect a force of Australian police attempting to restore civil rule there under threat from armed gangs.

High-tech warfare

Technology has transformed war. The face of war remains ugly, but modern, digitised warfare seems to promise a speedy end to conflicts and some reduction in human suffering. Guided missiles could well be the principal weapon of the future, directed to their target by computer operators thousands of kilometres from the war zone. Some visionaries even predict 'wars without casualties' in which infrastructure would be targeted and lives spared. In the Gulf Wars against Iraq (and in Afghanistan), air power destroyed enemy air strength, radar and communications sites, command posts, bases, military traffic and even power sources in order to reduce casualties in the ground forces. When the armies moved, they did so at night using infra-red that turned 'night into day'. The world hopes that America uses its vast armed power wisely.

Faithful allies: US President George W. Bush meets with Australian Prime Minister John Howard in the Oval Office of the White House in Washington DC.

Glossary

Allied member of alliance that fought Germany in both World Wars; British Empire, Russia, United States, France

armistice a cease-fire, usually followed by a peace treaty

atomic nuclear weapons

Axis enemy powers in the Second World War of 1939–45 ('Rome-Berlin-Tokyo Axis')

Berlin Wall wall built by Communist government of East Germany to prohibit its citizens leaving for the West

colonies overseas possessions of a European power

Communist political party that ruled Russia 1917–91 and took power in China in 1949; committed to the overthrow of capitalism

democratic nations with governments elected by the people, notable for their belief in personal freedom for their citizens

garrison army camp or base

genocide mass murder of people by a government

globalisation development in the world since the end of the tensions of the Cold War to internationalise economies, banking, trade

guerilla rebel or insurgent

infrastructure a nation's communications and constructions that form a basis for its defence (telephones, electricity, roads, airfields, command centres, etc.)

moratoriums pause (as in waging war or in debt payments)

Nazi Adolf Hitler's National Socialist extremist party that ruled Germany 1933–45, notable for its brutality, racism and militarism

neutralism uncommitted to any side in war

recession economic downturn

Red Communist

stalemate deadlock

totalitarian form of government that exerts total control over its people's lives, such as Nazi Germany and Communist Russia

veto a negative vote

West, the nations of Western Europe and Britain, or nations springing from the Western European tradition of democracy and tolerance, such as the United States, Canada, Australia and New Zealand; invariably opposed to totalitarian regimes

Index